MARTIAL ARTS
TUTORIAL SERIES

Multiple opponent combat
with one handed weapons

"Truth is ever to be found in simplicity,
and not in the multiplicity
and confusion of things"

Isaac Newton

Acknowledgements:

A huge heartfelt thanks to the following people whose time, patience and support were invaluable in putting together this tutorial:

Andrea Scheler

Patrick Scheler

Stefan Fisel

Sebastian Neckel

Frederico Martins

Florian Kiefer

Dragan Milojevic

What it has to offer

As a PE teacher turned coach, I believe sports should enrich trainees' lives.

This relying on quality practice, ***Training Answers*** is an info source on:

- ✔ Conditioning

- ✔ Teaching strategies

- ✔ Sport-specific skill
  (technique and tactical skill)

Study items currently available *(through Amazon)* and in project:

			WHAT to practice[1]	WHEN to practice[2]	HOW to practice[3]
MARTIAL SKILL **Stick fighting & fencing arts series**	**ONE ON ONE**	Tactics	DVD - **AVAILABLE**	Volume 1(book) **AVAILABLE**	Volume 2 TBA
		Technique	TBA	TBA	TBA
	MULTIPLE OPPONENTS		Book - Tutorial for one handed weapons		**AVAILABLE**
	Historical analysis		DVD evolution of Jogo do Pau's skillset, and its transfer to historical fencing		**AVAILABLE**
COACHING FOUNDATION	CONDITIONING		Book - TBA		
	TEACHING STRATEGIES		Book		**AVAILABLE**

---

[1] Systematization of contents.

[2] Organization of practice *(curriculum)*.

[3] Practice strategies *(pedagogical progressions, plus error assessment and corrective strategies)*.

TABLE OF CONTENTS

Introduction

Subject & target audience

Welcome to the first volume of *Training Answer's* **tutorial series on martial training**.

This first volume aims to serve all martial artists interested in an easy-to-use **training** tool that teaches **how to fight multiple opponents** while **wielding one handed weapons** (both blunt and bladed).

This skill set shall be presented using the baton, a blunt one handed weapon without a handguard. Nevertheless, engaging multiple opponents equally spread over a wide angle[4] presents outnumbered combatants with a very important **tactical constraint**:

The need to strike at multiple foes using swinging actions of high range of motion.

(linear/thrusting type strikes threaten only one foe at a time, thus allowing other foes to approach and attack while engaging only one foe)

As a result, **this tactical constraint** forces outnumbered combatants to **rely on swinging actions**.

This, in turn, means that the **skillset** which will be demonstrated using a baton is **equally valid** to those interested in **bladed (one handed) weapons**.

---

[4] That can easily vary between 45 and 360 degrees.

Presentation format

Most people involved in sports and martial arts lack the conditions to dedicate themselves professionally to these activities.

Related to this or not, I find that **many** individuals seem to be mainly **interested in** reaping the **results** of training, without forcefully feeling the need to understand the process, or even manage it. As someone who also looks for the mere treatment protocol when ill, I find that such search for training straight forwardness is both **logical and reasonable**.

Additionally, like many others of today's martial arts communities, I am of the belief that one does not need to master a whole system in order to know how to fight.

In light of this, I looked to organize this tutorial so as to **supply** a simple **training formula** to **trainees** interested in weapon combat, consisting of straight forward **drills** dully **organized into a** thorough **curriculum**.

In doing so, I **privileged tactics over technique**. This means that I took the liberty of presenting a selected group of techniques that allows for a learning experience that builds **a complete tactical system** for outnumbered combat. In practical terms, the focus is on supplying a simplified but thorough skill set to readers, and one that allows them **to immediately handle sparring** against multiple opponents.

After covering the main concepts that make up this particular combat strategy, the information pertaining the actual training of the skill set is divided into **three sections**[5]:
a) *fundamentals*, **b)** *combat skills* and **c)** *transfer to self-defence.*

---

[5] The 2nd section, which focuses on the learning of new movement patterns, includes photos for both right and left handers. The 1st and 3rd sections, being about concepts such as distance and tactical manoeuvring of multiple foes (and not about biomechanics), are shown using a right handed performer.

Though notes will be added regarding pedagogical information that is complementary to the exercises presented, individual analysis by a competent instructor can be very beneficial and should, therefore, be sought whenever available.

Regarding the "backstory" of the contents that will be shared, two introductory notes are in order, one pertaining to the martial labelling of these contents and another concerning the fundamental traits of this combat strategy.

STUDY MATERIAL

Discount code available on final pages

The martial labelling of this skill set

I learnt the fundamental core that makes up this outnumbered combat skillset while training Jogo do Pau under grandmaster Nuno Russo. Therefore, those interested in labelling these contents by identifying them with a specific art should use the label Jogo do Pau.

Personally, however, I have been experiencing progressively greater difficulty in relating to such labels. As a result, I feel that the nature of these contents is more effectively communicated using the designation *outnumbered combat with one handed weapons*, which is even useful in also conveying how this skill set can easily fit into the training of martial artists with different backgrounds. Here are my main reasons for preferring this designation.

15

First of all, I feel that there is not a single pure martial system in the world, in the sense that all trainees come to experience the exact same practice. The main reason for this is simple: martial practices are made alive by instructors and students, and no two instructors or students are the same, nor do they stay the same over their life span.

A good example of this is, I believe, that of karate, which branched out into different styles. However, even within each style, each instructor also has his or her own teaching fingerprint, which is responsible for conveying a different martial experience to students of, supposedly, the same style. Therefore, how different can two martial practices be in order to be considered part of the same style? And how similar must they be to be a part of the same art family? *(like karate)* Such borders are quite confusing to me, which is why I prefer to refer to the skillset being shared as *outnumbered combat with one handed weapons.*

Nevertheless, since some might still perceive this to be pure **Jogo do Pau** *(whatever that is)*, here are two additional thoughts to consider.

First, France used to have a system with the same name *(Jeux du Baton)*, in which both the weapon and the techniques used in duelling were the same as those used in Jogo do Pau. As is the case nowadays[6], countries interacted, meaning that this skill set might actually constitute the preservation of an ancient combat system from central Europe.

Secondly, when analysing combat regarding its different distances and resulting techniques, one even comes to realize that martial practices do not vary that much worldwide. On this topic, I perceive the practice of combat to entail three major distances:

✓ <u>**Long distance**</u>
> ➢ Where one uses a weapon that extends the reach of fighters

---

[6] Where communication promotes learning and transfer to occur between different schools of thought, and the concept of mma replacing the initial view of "pure" *(independent)* combat systems.

✓ **Medium distance**
  ➢ Where one strikes with the limbs extended *(kicks and jab type punches)*

✓ **Short distance**
  ➢ Where one is limited to grappling and short range striking techniques *(head butting, elbow and knee strikes, etc)*

There are many different combat sports, with each competitive setting usually being specialized in one of these three distances. The latter means that, depending on the competitive setting, fighters are only allowed to score points by using offensive manoeuvres from one of these three distances.

Combat outside of a sportive setting represents, however, the origin of martial arts: self-defence. This form of combat can easily involve a transition between distances, which can be systematized in the following manner:

✓ **Increase of distance**
  ➢ During the verbal conflict stage, it is possible to push away an opponent, when felt that it is advantageous to get to a wider combat distance

✓ **Shortening of combat distance**
  ➢ During a physical confrontation, where at least one of the fighters is aggressive, combat distance naturally shortens[7]

Concerning the latter, the shortening of combat distance, it is relevant to highlight the following elements:

---

[7] Constantly showcased in boxing bouts, where fighters consistently end up in a clinch.

> ➤ It can be temporarily avoided by side stepping

> ➤ It can only be comprehensively solved by seriously hurting the opponent who is consistently looking to shorten distance

> ➤ It happens very rapidly

Looking closer at the speed at which distance shortening occurs, the so called medium distance is not really an independent combat distance. This means that combatants do not exchange medium distance blows for a lengthy time frame, as commonly portrayed by some movies. Medium distance is, instead, a transitional distance when moving from long-range to short-range combat, where fighters get one shot at stopping their opponent.

Ultimately, what does this all mean?

The distance dependency of fighting is not country specific nor even continent specific. Consequently, it is not a surprise that both western and eastern fighting styles are, conceptually, the same:

> *The core made up by techniques for long (weapon) distance together with techniques for short (grappling) distance*

This core is then complemented with techniques for the transitional medium range. In rare cases medium range engagement brings either immediate victory – e.g by knock-out – or a slight advantage going into grappling – e.g. by hurting the opponent during the approach that leads to the clinch. Although sometimes useful, the medium range add-on is not fully reliable, which makes it inadequate to be used as the only tool in one's arsenal[8].

All in all, the possibility of Jogo do Pau being the preservation of something that extends beyond the borders of Portugal and, furthermore, the universal distance based logic that can be used in looking at combat systems all over the world, makes martial labelling increasingly confusing to me. But then again, perhaps it is just me, and I fully respect whatever labelling you choose, as the development of the actual skill set is what matters most to me.

Specifics of this outnumbered combat strategy

The previous rationale that depicts *martial* combat as a phenomenon where distance tends to be shortened corresponds, in a nutshell, to what people have come to know as mma *(mixed martial arts)* … only with the addition of weapons and without the many safety oriented rules that the latter has embraced over the years.

Consequently, I find it likely that readers might well expect a manual on outnumbered combat consisting of exactly that: A mixed long and short distance combat system for fighting multiple opponents.

Nevertheless, that will not be the case, as the system that will be shared focuses on long distance techniques. Before you classify this as an incoherence on my part, please read through the following rationale.

As stated by world-renown self-defence expert Geoff Thompson, grappling distance is the one distance fighters get locked into, meaning that the chances of moving *(from grappling)* back into wider combat distances are slim at best. Thompson also makes a point that, even in the case of being able to throw an opponent, the latter frequently exhibits a very strong grip that results in holding on to the clothes of

---

[8] Combat systems centered on medium range techniques *(under the premise that combat consists of several strikes being exchanged within this distance)*, were developed mostly in times of peace, when the focus of practice shifted from raw effectiveness to specialized recreation.

the thrower and pulling him or her to the ground. While all of this might be quite acceptable when faced with a single opponent, being locked in vertical grappling or pulled down to ground fighting is anything but ideal when facing multiple opponents who aggressively attack simultaneously. The safest way to use grappling in outnumbered combat might consist of holding on to an opponent in order to use the latter as hostage. Outside of this scenario, grappling should be deemed as non-ideal for outnumbered combat and, therefore, a solution within wider *(striking)* combat distances should be sought.

Still, this only means that grappling is non-ideal, and not that it will not happen, nor that one should neglect it in training. Therefore, why is it that the system which I shall be sharing with readers only covers wide distance combat? To understand this, let us analyse some important traits of striking arts in general and weapon combat arts in particular.

On the subject of striking arts, combatants' reach is one of its most influential variables. It is, therefore, without surprise that upon living in rural environments where spatial limitations were rare, people wisely began by focusing on two handed weapons. These weapons were, frequently, double the length of batons and walking canes.

Such longer weapons entail a wider combat distance and, therefore, a greater time window to react to foes looking to close distance. Furthermore, the difference in physical properties between wood and the human body means that a thick staff is capable of inflicting greater damage than a punch or a kick. All in all, using a 1,5m staff to fight off multiple opponents allows for great effectiveness at a distance, including the stoppage of foes looking to shorten combat distance.

Later on, as recent urban societies eliminated the staff from daily life, batons and walking canes gained greater relevance within the self-defence context. It can, therefore, be concluded that the outnumbered combat system for one handed weapons about to be shared had its origins in the longer two handed weapons … regardless of the label being Jogo do Pau or central European fencing.

Given this, it is only natural that grandmaster Nuno Russo approached the use of one handed weapons within outnumbered combat under the same distance centred approach, as it:

➤ Represented the application *(transference)* of the rationale grandmaster Russo was trained in and had experienced success in upon learning staff combat

➤ Answers the basic need of finding a long-range centred solution to outnumbered combat

Of course that the shortening of the weapon from a 1,5m staff to a 0,8m baton *(or even less)*, makes combat faster. Consequently, and in all honesty, this very effective and reliable wide-distance staff approach to outnumbered combat loses a bit of its reliability when using shorter weapons, with grappling having a better chance of occurring. Then, wouldn't it make sense for the system to develop a combination of long and short distance solutions?

For sure yes … but only if functional.

On this subject, here are the main limitations for developing a striking-grappling hybrid system for outnumbered combat:

➤ As previously stated, the successful application of grappling to outnumbered combat is frequently limited to using a foe as a hostage … itself very difficult should the hostage be of similar or greater physical stature *(strength)*

➤ Tools are, most times, context specific, and the potential use of striking weapons in grappling is very limited.

In short, putting together an add-on of baton grappling for outnumbered combat makes as much sense as putting together an add-on of gun grappling. Therefore, I decided against putting together a hybrid system I do not believe in, just to improve the potential marketing of the product by accommodating it to the mma trend. I will, instead, be sharing a tool that, like any other tool, is not perfect and much less infallible. However, and despite this, it does have combat tested strengths that can represent a great asset when used according to its core strategy. Simply put, just like with firearms, one should focus on maximizing effectiveness at a distance when wielding one handed weapons. Otherwise, using such weapons to grapple either brings defeat or, at the very least, eliminates the major advantage of having such weapons.

Those looking to merge this outnumbered combat distance centred approach with some sort of grappling safety net, thus creating a personal hybrid, will naturally follow such path. Nevertheless, for such process to develop with quality and martial soundness, I will limit my input to the field I am most experienced in, while urging those seeking this route to get complementary instruction from an expert grappling instructor. Remember, however, to "test-drive" such hybrid in training using free sparring against non-compliant test partners, best found amongst those who do not train your system.

As this brings an end to the major introductory concepts I felt were relevant to share, let us now move on to the fun and important sections dedicated to the analysis and training of this skill set.

Luís Preto, MSc

A combat strategy for outnumbered combat

*"When facing multiple opponents,
you must attack first and keep attacking
until the danger subdues"*

Miyamoto Musashi

"Know the other and know yourself;
one hundred challenges without danger"

Step 1: Profiling the combat behaviour displayed by groups

One simple way of classifying one's foes consists of splitting them into:

1) Experienced skilled combatants

2) Inexperienced unskilled combatants

Unsurprisingly, unskilled foes can be overcome using simple strategies that fail to show the same degree of effectiveness against skilled foes. More to the point, unskilled foes commonly display the following behaviours:

➢ Attacking one at a time

➢ Either approaching their opponent from the same direction, or allowing the outnumbered combatant to line them up

Strategies such as lining up opponents can, indeed, start by being one's first training stage. Nevertheless, it can be very dangerous to limit one's training to strategies that work only against unskilled opponents. It is, instead, wiser to assume that such opponents will usually be eliminated through *natural selection* and, consequently, focus the training process on developing functional strategies for dealing with skilled opponents … which is what this book looks to offer.

On the limited effectiveness of lining up one's foes, do not take my word for it. Perform, instead, the following test game.

In a scenario of 2 against 1, the lone player scores one point each time he or she successfully manages to line up the two opponents in front of him / her. The team of two players scores a point each time either one manages to touch the back of the lone opponent.

Should the strategy of lining up opponents prove to be easy, then the teams of two players will be consistently defeated by their opponent.

Simply put, the system that shall be shared looks to supply readers with tools meant to overcome opponents who:

1) Look to surround the outnumbered combatant, sometimes doing so cunningly from the very beginning

2) Resist being lined up

3) Approach and attack simultaneously from different directions

*"Attack is the secret of defence,
and defence is the planning of an attack"*

Sun Tzu

Step 2: The dual defensive action, the core strategical premise of outnumbered combat

In devising a skill set geared towards being successful in fighting multiple opponents, one needs to start by defining how to measure success within this combat scenario. To do so, forget about all the martial arts movies you have watched and all the hero centred martial arts choreographed exhibitions. Focus, instead, exclusively on your reliable good old friend common-sense when answering the following question:

When faced with multiple opponents of your skill level, do you believe it is easy or even doable to knock them all out and ride gloriously into the sunset?

The answer cannot be other than a clear and resounding NO!

That being the case, the fundamental GOAL is "simply" to survive outnumbered combat, where the odds of survival are highly unfavourable for the outnumbered combatant.

For that effect, no scenario has a greater success/survival rate than to avoid conflicts altogether. Therefore, common-sense naturally dictates that the primary strategies should be that of:

1) Avoiding places where conflicts are more likely

2) Running away from potential outnumbered combat scenarios

When, however, one is unable to avoid outnumbered combat, by getting ambushed or having escape-routs blocked, an additional strategy is needed in order to guide the actions of the outnumbered combatant during actual combat.

As pinpointed in the previous profiling of the behaviour exhibited by groups of skilled assailants, the combat strategy of the outnumbered combatant needs to succeed in allowing him or her to:

***Continuously avoid strikes from opponents
approaching from multiple directions,
while looking for a way to escape.***

Therefore, even in actual combat, the focus is a defensive one. Case in point, preserving one's physical integrity long enough to run away, instead of focusing on beating down all foes.

However, how can one protect oneself from more than one opponent approaching and attacking from different directions, when in the possession of only one weapon? The answer is, by making use of the two defensive tools at everyone's disposal:

➢ The weapon

➢ Distance

In practical terms, such dual defensive action plays out in the following manner:

Choosing one direction to move towards,
in order to use the weapon for coverage from strikes;
while moving out of the remaining foes' reach.

This concept then "merely" warrants repetitive application in different directions, so that foes are continuously kept at bay … until one is finally able to escape.

Should opponents make mistakes that expose them to being hit *(as this defensive minded offensive strategy is performed)*, the outnumbered combatant can and should exploit such opportunities. The overall combat strategy is not, however, built around expecting such mistakes by opponents, since one cannot control *(much less predict)* the skill level of one's opponents.

Lastly, this operational definition concerning the strategy for outnumbered combat is important in rebutting a very common criticism. The latter states that this type of combat practice is unrealistic, as the combatants forming the group of assailants seem to passively wait for the lone combatant to attack them. The thing is that, when the outnumbered combatant skilfully manages to steal the initiative and does not relinquish it, the foes making up the group of assailants are kept in a reactive role. As a result, the combatants forming the group of assailants have to constantly readjust their positioning, given the ability of the outnumbered combatant to continuously and unpredictably change both his or her positioning and distance towards each combatant of the group of assailants. Therefore, the opponents of the outnumbered combatant see their attempts at attacking inhibited by pre-emptive strikes from latter, as they get pre-emptively attacked when trying to close distance in order to get their opponent within reach.

It is, therefore, my hope that this document will succeed in conveying the validity of this approach and, consequently, get its readers to fully understand and value the beauty of this simple, yet functional, martial skill set.

Specifications of the dual defensive action

As just mentioned, one uses the weapon for defensive coverage when approaching foes positioned in a given direction. There are, however, two different ways to do so:

➤ Parrying the foe's strike, and then countering it

➤ Inhibiting the foe's strike through a pre-emptive strike

Between these two strategies, the second is deemed more reliable and thus preferable, since the performance of a strike requires less skill than that of parrying and countering.

Summary

The operational definition concerning the strategy for outnumbered combat can be summarized through the following 3 points:

1. Steal the initiative *(the active role)* from the opponents, thus relegating them to a reactive roll[9]

2. Strike by moving towards foes in a given direction, thus stepping away from the remaining foes

3. Continuously keep the opponents at bay through sequences of unpredictable strikes in different directions *(together with constant displacement)*

The reason **why this strategy works** is:

➢ **Opponents** are **also** made of flesh. This means that they also **bleed and die**, which leads them to react defensively when attacked

➢ Like anyone else **reacting defensively**, distancing oneself on defence also proves to be more

STUDY MATERIAL

A complete analysis behind counter attack selection in duelling, and its training

Discount code available on final pages

---

[9] This requires one (1) to be aware of one's environment in order to detect a threat (which system works after having a bottle smashed on the head from behind?), (2) to be capable of reading when a situation escalates into an unavoidable physical conflict, best overcome by means of a pre-emptive strike.

reliable for the group of assailants, compared to parrying on the same spot[10]

➢ In turn, this entails **having to perform a re-approaching step** in order to reach the outnumbered combatant **with a counter**, which is crucial in giving the latter enough **space**, and **thus time, to handle multiple assailants**

Of course that, **when** presented with **foes** who **fail to exit**, it is **crucial** to find a way of **punishing them**, otherwise their counter strike from a closer starting distance may prove to be too fast to handle.

The use of pre-emptive strikes will always be dependent of one's judgement, which is obviously error prone. Being sure of what a situation requires of someone merely entails a reaction, not a decision between different options. Such reactions, though very accurate, come at the price of being too late in order to avoid defeat. Making an earlier decision between different options includes uncertainty, hence the chance of some bad calls. That **is just the nature of things, and there is no way around it**. When in charge of such decisions, it is awesome if one manages to choose a response based on roughly 70% of the information concerning the problem *(as pointed out by American General Colin Powell)*. As for the possibility of sometimes overreacting within the specific context of self-defence, Geoff Thompson's quote *"It is better to be judged by 12 than carried by 6"* might make sense to some of you. **From a legal standpoint** *(regarding the use of pre-emptive strikes in self-defence situations)*, you need to **check your own law system**. However, in many cases the law seems to allow for pre-emptive strikes, as long as you were in distress *(which one always is when confronted with*

---

[10] Given that in unprotected combat one has but one life, the fear / respect brought about by an aggressive outnumbered combatant who steals the initiative (by performing punishing strikes through unpredictable trajectories and displacements) usually gets foes to back off.

several foes) and did not seek the conflict, which will for sure be the case should you be on the right side of the force.

From this clear understanding of the challenges placed by outnumbered combat and the strategy that is to be performed in opposition to it, let us move on to the actual training of this skill set, in the form of its technique and tactical applications.

Outnumbered combat: Training program

"Simplicity is the ultimate sophistication"

Leonardo da Vinci

Terminology – Introductory note

Writing a tutorial to serve both right and left handers motivated the use of a terminology that differs from that of referring to combatants' left or right side of the body.

Therefore, the terminology that shall be used is as follows:

1. Based on the terminology present in racket sports, the terms forehand and backhand side are used frequently, with:

    a. The forehand side being the side of the hand holding the weapon, which is the right side in the case of right handers and the left side in the case of lefties

    b. The backhand side being the side opposite to the side of the hand holding the weapon

2. In certain cases *(such as when referring to the legs)*, where the use of the terms forehand and backhand side is uncommon, the terms dominant side and non-dominant side are also used. Considering that the dominant side corresponds to the most skilled side *(used for tasks such as writing)*:

    a. The dominant side is the same as forehand side, case in point, the right side for right handers and the left side for left handers

    b. The non-dominant side is the same as backhand side, case in point, the left side for right handers and the right side for left handers

Here is a short summary that will, hopefully, make this easy to follow:

	Terminology 1	Terminology 2	Side
Right handers	Forehand	Dominant	Right
	Backhand	Non-dominant	Left
Left handers	Forehand	Dominant	Left
	Backhand	Non-dominant	Right

Coaching info:

To practice this program as an add-on to one's regular martial practice:

☞ *Practice each lesson twice per week over 2 weeks (30 minutes each time)*
  ✓ *1st week for familiarization with the new contents*
  ✓ *2nd week for refinement and consolidation*

The organization of the skill set (from simple to complex) promotes the continued retention of previously trained skills as new contents are added.

At 5 months one full go at the program is done. A second go should follow for refinement, especially regarding sparring application.

Stage 1: Development of starting fundamentals

Lesson 1: Initial distance

Goal: To establish a standard self-defence starting position.

Exercise 1 – variation A

1. In pairs, trainee A holds a baton and trainee B is empty handed

2. Trainee A adopts a combat stance:

> Holding the baton with the dominant hand on the forehand side (at waist height), and directing it towards the opponent

> Placing the dominant leg forward (the leg on the side of the baton)

3. Trainee B then looks to grab the front tip of the baton, in order to render it useless

**Exercise 1
Variation A**

1 Starting position

2 Unarmed trainee tries to grab baton

3 Unarmed trainee succeeds

Critical variable:

Weapon held too close to opponent

4. Trainee B scores a point for every success

Coaching info:

The critical variables that determine the degree of success in avoiding having the baton grabbed by the opponent are:

1) Initial distance

*2) Speed of reaction to the opponent's approach
(by stepping back, in order to maintain distance)*

Trainees need to (1) ensure they position themselves in a standard wide starting distance after each repetition (as the attacker shortens distance on every repetition), and then (2) react as quickly as possible to their opponent.

After 10 attempts, trainees should switch roles

Exercise 1 – variation B

1. Repeat the exercise while having the armed trainee placing the non-dominant leg in front (the leg on the side opposite to the baton), thus holding the baton further back than on variation A

Exercise 1
Variation B

1 Starting position

2 Unarmed trainee tries to grab baton

3 Unarmed trainee fails

Critical variable:

Weapon held further away from opponent

2. Compare the degree of success experienced in both exercises, using such analysis to determine which leg should be placed, by rule of thumb, in a lead position.

> **Coaching info:**
>
> *Given the baton is, in variation B, placed further back from the very beginning, grabbing the baton should prove to be more difficult.*
>
> *Consequently, combatants should conclude that the baton ought to be held further back within self-defence settings, by means of placing the non-dominant leg forward.*
>
> *This obviously includes the context of outnumbered combat.*

Exercise 1 – variation C

Repeat variation B, with the armed trainee being allowed to score points by attacking when managing distance

> **Coaching info:**
>
> *This includes striking when exiting, but it also includes striking before the opponent even tries to grab the baton. The latter should be used especially when the unarmed trainee looks to shorten the initial distance before attempting to grab the baton.*
>
> *For safe maximum speed / contact training, appropriate adapted weapons and protective gear need to be used.*

Exercise 1
Variation C

1 Starting position

2 Unarmed trainee tries to grab baton

3 Armed trainee exits while initiating a strike

Critical variables:

Starting distance

Exercise 1
Variation C

4 Back swing of weapon

5 Forward release of strike

6 Strike connecting with opponent

Critical variable:

Reach advantage

Lesson 2: Reach and footwork

Goal:

To become familiarized with the reach allowed by batons and, at the same time, effectively manage approaching steps accordingly.

Introductory note

When finishing a strike, the upper limb is close to full extension.

In developing this skill set, it is important for trainees to get acquainted with the new reach enabled by these weapons. Furthermore, this need is made even more relevant by the fact that the visual reference concerning the baton in its starting position (*next to the hip*) may lead trainees to wrongly assume this to be their striking reach (*and, consequently, hinder their ability to protect themselves as a result of approaching excessively*).

Exercise 2 – variation A

1. Trainees start by positioning themselves far from each other. Such distance should require anything from one to several steps, for either combatant to get into striking reach

2. The armed trainee should:
   - ☞ Extend the upper limb forward
   - ☞ Approach the training partner and, by relying on the visual reference supplied by the weapon, interrupt the approach

as soon as the lead tip of the baton reaches the training partner

3. At the end of each repetition, the trainee serving as a target should step back. The goal is to set up another repetition, while deliberately and constantly supplying the trainee who is approaching varying starting distances.

    ☞ The attacker should wait for the training partner to finish the distancing step before starting another approach

**Exercise 2
Variation A**

1 Starting
position

2 Armed
trainee
performing
the
approaching
step

3 Armed
finishing
approaching
step

*Critical
variable:*

*Awareness
of reach*

**Exercise 2
Variation A**

1 Starting position (wider)

2 Armed trainee extends upper limbs

3 Armed trainee performs first step

Critical variable:

Awareness of stride length

**Exercise 2
Variation A**

4 Transition between 1st and 2nd approaching steps

5 Final stages of 2nd approaching step

6 End of approach

Critical variable:

Reach awareness

Exercise 2
Variation A

1 Wide starting position

2 Armed trainee extends upper limb

3 Narrow approaching step

Critical variables:

Awareness of reach & stride length

Exercise 2
Variation A

4 End of 2nd step

5 Final stages of 3rd step

6 End of 3rd approaching step

Critical variables:

Awareness of reach & stride length

Exercise 2 – variation B

As stated already, there is a difference in reach between the starting position *(with the weapon held next to the hip)* and the end position of the strike.

With this in mind, trainees ought to perform the following exercise:

1. Repeat the previous exercise while approaching with the baton held in the standard starting position

2. Stop the approach upon reaching their personal striking reach, thus leaving a gap between the weapon and the opponent

3. After finishing the approach, trainees should check their distance, in order to ensure that they did stop their approach within their proper striking reach[11]

---

[11] Reaching the target with the lead tip of the weapon, and the elbow close to full extension.

**Exercise 2
Variation B**

1 Approach with weapon held next to hip

2 Finishing approach at one's real striking reach

3 Checking reach *(success in managing approach)*

Critical variable:

Awareness of reach

> ## Coaching info:
>
> *Whenever the approach is incorrect (by either approaching in excess or not enough), the approaching trainee should correct his or her distance to the target before the trainee serving as a target starts moving back (to set up another repetition). This naturally entails:*
>
> ➢ *Approaching more (an extra half step, or a full step even), when the initial approach was insufficient*
>
> ➢ *Stepping slightly back (with the foot that was moved forward) when the approach was excessive*
>
> *Additionally, when needing to approach more, it is common for trainees to raise their back heel and lean forward. For reasons to do with balance and the ability to react quickly to the opponent's counter move, this should be avoided. As stated, an additional half or full step should be performed in such cases, while maintaining both heels firmly on the ground.*

Exercise 2 – variation C

This time, everything should be put together, by approaching while also striking.

1. When starting from a very wide distance, it does not make sense to begin the strike together with the start of the approaching step. Instead, one should look to approach with the weapon placed in the starting position, until reaching the distance from where the opponent can be reached by taking just one additional step

2. Upon reaching this one-step distance, the armed trainee should perform the final step together with the strike

Exercise 2
Variation C

1 Starting
position

2 1st stage:
*Approach
to get to
striking
reach*

3 End of 1st
stage

***Critical
variable:***

*Awareness
of real
offensive
reach*

(Again, it should be the trainee serving as a target to distance him or herself between repetitions)

**Exercise 2
Variation C**

4 Start of 2nd stage: *Strike with approach*

5 Halfway point of 2nd stage

6 End of strike

Critical variables:

Awareness of reach, stride length and strike duration

Lesson 3: Pre-emptive striking

Goal: To introduce the concept and timing of pre-emptive strikes.

Exercise 3 – variation A

Repeat the previous exercise *(variation C of exercise 2)* with the following change:

➤ As the trainee with the baton starts the forward release of the strike, the trainee serving as target takes a step back, in order to avoid being reached by the strike

☞ Given the wider combat distance characteristic of weapon combat, it is advisable to exit by means of a back step with the lead leg

Exercise 3 – variation B

1. The trainee who is approaching continues to do so in order to get into striking distance and, if allowed, performs a strike

2. The other trainee, now also holding a weapon, will look to pre-emptively strike the approaching trainee. To do so successfully, the following timing needs to be performed:

☞ The trainee being approached needs to step forward with a *(pre-emptive)* strike on the second to last approaching step of the opponent. Perhaps more simply put, as the latter performs the last approaching with the baton held in the starting position *(before initiating the attacking motion)*

☞ For starters, a pre-emptive strike should be performed on the forehand side

<u>Coaching info</u>:

As stated, the approaching trainee should still approach with the goal of attacking.

Therefore, whenever the trainee who is being approached leaves the pre-emptive strike too late, the approaching trainee should strike.

In such cases, the trainee being approached should react with the distancing step trained in variation A of this exercise.

**Exercise 3
Variation B**

2 Approach to get to striking reach

3 Left side trainee finishing approach. Right side trainee strikes pre-emptively

4 End of strike

Critical variables:

Timing strike with opponent's approaching steps

Exercise 3 – variation C

➤ Repetition of variation B, while performing a pre-emptive strike on the backhand side

**Exercise 3
Variation C**

2 Approach to get to striking reach

3 Left side trainee finishing approach. Right side trainee strikes pre-emptively

4 End of strike

Critical variables:

Timing strike with opponent's approaching

Lesson 4: Immediate threat on the forehand side

Goal: To apply the concepts of distance management and pre-emptive striking to outnumbered combat.

Exercise 4: Engagement strike on forehand side

1. Two combatants approach the outnumbered combatant, while looking to surround the latter

2. For learning purposes, the combatant located on the side of the weapon of the lone combatant approaches first

3. From the standard self-defence starting position *(with the non-dominant leg placed forward)*, the outnumbered combatant reacts with a pre-emptive strike. Such strike is performed:

   ➤ Inside-out[12], which translates into a strike on the backhand side

      ☞ Plus, by rule of thumb, resorting to a diagonal descending trajectory

   ➤ Together with an approaching step with the back leg

---

[12] Inside-out means that, having the performer of the strike as reference, the strike is performed from the centre line of the body to the periphery *(proximal-distal, using the terminology of anatomical studies)*.

> ## Coaching info:
>
> *It is not that uncommon for beginners to strike using an outside-in striking motion (striking to the forehand side with a forehand strike), as doing so seems to fit more naturally with the approaching step.*
>
> *In more complex settings, where one faces more than two opponents, doing so fails to threaten foes positioned in front of the lone combatant, thus allowing them to easily approach.*
>
> *To prepare for such cases, trainees need to ensure that the engagement strike is a backhand strike towards the opponent on the forehand / dominant side.*

Exercise 4, solo demo – Starting position

Exercise 4
Solo demo

2 Swing on backhand side, and approach with back leg

3 Pre-emptive strike

4 End of strike

Critical variable:

Striking inside-out

Exercise 4 Partner demo

2 Left side opponent approaches

3 "Stealing" initiative to the forehand side

4 End of strike

Critical variable:

Timing strike with approach of opponent

On the use of pre-emptive strikes

In accordance with the strategical concepts previously outlined, the engagement strike needs to include enough variability that it keeps the opponents guessing and, therefore, respectful enough of the strike that they react with the more reliable distancing step *(in comparison to parrying on the same spot)*. Therefore:

➢ The outnumbered combatant needs to vary the height of the strike *(punishing the lead knee of the opponent)*, should the latter look to aggressively parry without exiting.

☞ Added variability is possible by performing a swinging uppercut, also from inside-out, upon stealing the initiative. This option can prove to be especially useful against foes capable of parrying the legs, as the absence of any sort of handguard makes the outnumbered combatant's hand highly vulnerable.

Within self-defence settings, one usually faces foes who are ignorant as to the pre-emptive striking approach of this system. Furthermore, the numerical advantage they hold over the lone combatant also tends to heighten their aggressiveness. This to say that it is quite common for the combatants forming the group of assailants to approach rather carelessly *(without any defensive concern)* and, as a result:

It is normal for the first strike to effectively hit the assailant one decides to attack first.

Consequently, the overall impact of the first strike should be maximized through aggressive posturing, so as to hopefully intimidate the remaining assailants.

Exercise 5: Follow through after the engagement strike on the forehand side

After using the engagement strike to push away one opponent and increase distance towards the other, one should follow through with a pre-emptive strike towards the opponent one distanced him or herself from, and who is now approaching.

Doing so by maximizing movement flow entails performing the striking motion that is most easily available from the end position of the engagement strike.

In practical terms, this involves the following actions by the outnumbered combatant:

1. Turn the head to the opponent, by rotating it over the shoulder of the backhand side

2. Naturally follow with the turn of the shoulders which, in turn, ignites:

   ➤ A transition of the centre of gravity from the dominant leg to the non-dominant leg

   ➤ A forehand strike from the shoulder, while starting to approach with a passing step

   ☞ The forehand strike is released during the transition of the centre of gravity, and concluded during the initial stages of the approaching step.

74

> ## Coaching info:
>
> *This technique entails 2 strikes and only 1 step forward.*
>
> *When first trying out this technique, it is normal for trainees to perform it very slow, as they are looking to avoid mistakes. However, this tends to have the weapon artificially moving much slower than the step. This results in performing the full approaching step on the first strike and, afterwards, an undesirable second step with the second strike.*
>
> *This is a common mistake that trainees should be on the look-out for. One useful strategy in avoiding this entails the following 3 stage practice:*
>
> 1. *Start by practicing the 2 strike combination without footwork*
> 2. *Follow by practicing the footwork: step, turn, step, turn, etc*
> 3. *Merge the 2 strike combination with the footwork*
>
> *Upon finishing the double strike combination, the outnumbered combatant should look at the other opponent (the one attacked with the engagement strike), and perform the same double strike (pre-emptive) combination.*

3. Immediately follow with a second strike

   ➢ This is accomplished by swinging the weapon on the backhand side, while performing the approaching step with the back leg

Exercise 5
Solo demo

1 End position of 1st strike

2 Squaring off with opposite foe

3 Release of strike to opposite foe

Critical variable:

Release of strike before step

Exercise 5
Solo demo

4 End of strike and start of approach

5 Approach with release of follow through strike

6 End of double strike combination

Critical variables:

Two strike and only one step

Exercise 5
Solo demo

7 Start of 2nd double strike combination

8 Start of second strike *(and approach)*

9 End of double strike combination

Critical variable:

Quickly flowing from one combination to the next

78

Exercise 5
Partner
demo

1 Following the 1st strike with a combination to the foe on the right

2 End of 1st strike of the two strike combination

3 Transition to the second strike of the combination

Critical variable:

Anticipate strikes from opponents

Exercise 5 Partner demo

4 End of second strike

5 Immediate transition to a two strike combination towards the foe on the left

6 End of first strike

Critical variable:

Anticipate strikes from opponents

Coaching info:

1. *The behaviour of the combatants forming the group of assailants should be as follows :*

    a. *When the outnumbered combatant is attacking a given opponent, the remaining opponents should step forward, looking to approach the lone combatant. Their goal should be to position themselves close enough to perform a strike*

        ☞ *Doing so can even help prevent the performance of two steps forward by the lone combatant, as the immediate pressure by an opponent elicits the release of the first strike during the turn / weight transference*

    b. *The combatants approaching should immediately stop and switch into a back step when the lone combatant changes the direction of his or her displacement (by starting to move in their direction with a pre-emptive strike)*

        ☞ *Again, the height of either strike should be varied, to keep opponents guessing and thus honest (stepping back) ... or punish them when they fail to exit*

Lesson 5: Reinforcement of combat variability

Goal: To add further variability within the exchanges, in order to promote defensive balance between combatants.

Introductory note

As one trains the previous drill, it is normal for the combatants forming the group of assailants to realize the pattern being performed and, as a result, start gambling on their prediction of double strike combinations being continuously performed in alternate directions.

As result, combatants usually start approaching the lone combatant sooner, in anticipation of the double strike sequence in someone else's direction.

This occurrence allows for foes to approach sooner, presenting the outnumbered combatant with increasingly greater difficulty in being continuously successful at inhibiting strikes from the opponents *(by means of pre-emptive strikes).*

Consequently, we shall now add further combat variability, in order to reintroduce a better balance to this equation.

Doing so delays the start of the approaching steps by the combatants forming the group of assailants and, therefore, results in improving the ability of the lone combatant to keep the assailants at bay for a longer time frame.

Exercise 6: Variation between double strike combinations in one direction and in two different directions

1. The outnumbered combatant should start by repeating a double strike combination from the end position of the engagement strike *(towards the opponent standing in the direction opposite to that of the foe initially attacked with the engagement strike)*

2. Then, instead of performing a second double strike combination in full towards the foe attacked with the engagement strike, the outnumbered combatant should split two strikes between the foes in the following manner

    a. As is the case with the double strike combination previously trained, the outnumbered combatant performs a first strike *(with a half step)* in the direction of the foe approaching from behind

    b. As the outnumbered combatant chooses not to follow through with the second strike in the same direction, the approaching step is interrupted *(at a stage where the feet are next to each other – half a step)*

    c. From the end position of this first strike, the outnumbered combatant should turn the head and shoulders towards the other opponent. Such rotation of head and shoulders moves the weapon *(handle)* towards the opponent that the outnumbered combatant was moving away from. This results in a surprise strike from the shoulder on the backhand side, towards the assailant who was starting to approach from behind

        i. This strike is performed together with a half step towards that opponent *(with the dominant leg)*

**Exercise 6
Solo demo**

1 End of initial pre-emptive strike

2 Transition towards the other opponent

3 Strike towards foe on the right

Critical variable:

Stopping step with feet side by side

Exercise 6
Solo demo

4 Rotation of upper body

5 Release of strike to the left side

6 End of strike

Critical variable:

Step with same leg (dominant leg)

Exercise 6
Solo demo

7 Release of
1st strike,
*of the two
strike
combination*

8 End of
strike

9 Transition
between
strikes

***Critical
variable:***

*Strike before
stepping
forward*

Exercise 6
Solo demo

10 Release of 2nd strike, *of the two strike combination*

11 End of 2nd strike, *of the two strike combination*

Critical variable:

Identical first strike on both sequences keeps opponents guessing

Exercise 6 Partner demo

1 End of pre-emptive strike

2 release of 1st strike

**Exercise 6
Partner demo**

3 End of strike, *rotating towards the other foe*

4 Release of surprise strike towards foe on the left

5 End of strike

Critical variable:

Flow in changing direction

**Exercise 6
Partner
demo**

6 Release of
first strike

7 End of 1st
strike

8 Transition
between
strikes

*Critical
variable:*

*1st strike
without step*

**Exercise 6
Partner
demo**

9 End of
second
strike

10 Start of
strike to the
left

11 End of
strike

***Critical
variable:***

*Stop step
with feet
side by side*

**Exercise 6
Partner
demo**

12 Start of
strike
toward
opponent
on the right

13 End of
strike

14 First
strike of the
two strike
combination

**Exercise 6
Partner
demo**

15
Transition
between
strikes

16 Release
of second
strike

17 End of
first strike

***Critical
variable:***

*Identical 1st
strike keeps
opponents
guessing*

3. The outnumbered combatant should then repeat a few additional sets of this four strike sequence, which consists of:
    a. A double strike combination where the strikes are performed in opposite directions
    b. A double strike combination in the same direction

Exercise 7: Integration of skills

1. For additional training, the outnumbered combatant will now bring everything together by:

    a. Performing an engagement strike towards the forehand side *(with a backhand strike)*

    b. Following through with 3 sets of the 4 strike sequence
        i. A double strike combination in the same direction
        ii. A double strike combination split in opposite directions

Exercise 8: Preparation of free play

After starting, again, with the engagement strike, the outnumbered combatant will practice following through with 2 sets of these different combinations:

a) One double strike sequence in the same direction, followed by a one double strike sequence in opposite directions

b) Two double strike sequences[13], followed by one double strike sequence in opposite directions

c) Three double strike sequences, followed by one double strike sequence in opposite directions

Exercise 9: Free play

Use the combinations practiced in the previous exercise freely, thus randomly selecting the moment for performing the double strike sequence in opposite directions.

Coaching info:

Again, it is crucial for the outnumbered combatant to remember to continue varying the height of the strikes.

To facilitate this, each time the outnumbered combatant manages to land a strike on the knee of an opponent, the latter has to incur in some sort of punishment (such as 5 push ups), in order to make up for the fact that the controlled and safe training setting eliminates the risk of injury.

---

[13] Note, however, not to the same opponent. This means two strikes against opponent "A", followed by two strikes against opponent "B".

Lesson 6: Immediate threat on the backhand side, footwork A

Goal: To develop the pre-emptive engagement strike on the backhand side.

Exercise 10: Engagement strike on the backhand side

1. This time the opponent on the lone combatant's backhand side approaches first

2. To this, the outnumbered combatant reacts by performing a forehand diagonal descending strike

    a. Regarding footwork technique, an approach with the back leg is again performed.

        This time, however, one should not perform a full passing step with the back leg, since such action would force the outnumbered combatant to finish the strike with his or her back turned to the other opponent. Hence, the alternative footwork that is used in this case is that of a double half step, which entails bringing the back foot towards the lead foot and then the opposite foot back to its initial leading position.

        i. When performing the second half step, one does so by moving the lead leg diagonally *(not forward)*. Simply put, this second half of the footwork action is performed in the direction of the assailant being pre-emptively attacked.

Exercise 10
Solo demo

1 Starting position

2 First phase of strike, with approaching step *(using back leg)*

3 End of strike

Critical variable:

Diagonal step, to move away from the other foe

100

Coaching info:

When performing the first half step, one can do so by moving the foot straight forward or, alternatively, moving it behind the lead foot. Choosing between these two is done based on the positioning of the opponent one is approaching:

➤ *When the opponent on the backhand side is closer to the outnumbered combatant's centre line, the latter should simply move the back foot forward, in the direction of the opponent.*

➤ *When, however, the opponent on the backhand side is at a steeper angle towards the outside (further away from the centre line), the outnumbered combatant needs to move the back foot slightly behind the lead foot. By doing so, one successfully adapts the stepping motion to the fundamental concept of stepping straight towards the opponent.*

**Exercise 10
Partner
demo**

1 Starting
position,
*foe on the
right
approaches*

**Exercise 10
Partner
demo**

2 "Steal" the
initiative
*(pre-emptive
strike)*

3 Forward
release of
strike

4 End of first
strike

***Critical
variable:***

*Timing
approach by
foes,
strike hand if
reachable*

Lesson 7: Follow through strike to the forehand engagement strike, and its alternative footwork

Goal: To develop the follow through strike to the pre-emptive engagement strike on the backhand side.

Exercise 11: Follow through to the engagement strike

1. Upon finishing the forehand engagement strike towards the foe on the backhand side, the outnumbered combatant should turn the head and shoulders to the opponent on the forehand side

    a. In doing so, the following two changes should occur simultaneously:

        i. The baton is placed over the shoulder on the backhand side

        ii. The foot of the dominant / forehand side should be displaced towards the imaginary line that connects the two opponents. The latter means positioning oneself deliberately between the opponents.

            ☞ Depending on how far the opponent on the forehand side is, sometimes a slight lunge might also be needed *(to cover a wider distance)*

2. This should be immediately followed by a shoulder strike from the backhand side, towards the opponent on the forehand side

    a. As for footwork, the foot of the backhand / non dominant side should approach the lead foot and stop next to it *(half a step)*

3. Upon finishing the previous strike, the outnumbered combatant should square off with the opponent on the backhand side *(the one initially attacked)*, and follow through with a double strike combination towards that opponent: A forehand strike from the shoulder, followed with a swinging backhand strike

    a. Given the proximity of the opponent:

        i. The initial forehand strike from the shoulder should be released during the turn of the head/shoulders *(without any approaching footwork)*

        ii. The second strike of the combination *(the swinging strike on the backhand side)* should then follow, together with half a step forward with the dominant / forehand side leg

Exercise 12: Integration exercise

1. The outnumbered combatant will now practice the previous exercise *(engagement and follow through)*, together with the following sequences of additional strikes. These additional strikes are organized in sets of three combinations, as practiced before:

> A first double strike combination in one direction
> A second double strike combination in the opposite direction
> A third double strike combination, only this time split into one strike in each direction

Exercise 13: Engagement strike on the backhand side – footwork variation B

1. This time around, the outnumbered combatant will allow for the opponent to approach a bit more.

   ➤ Note, however, that this should be avoided in combat, since such close distance might very easily allow for the approaching assailant to steal the initiative.

   It is, however, beneficial to get acquainted with this different scenario, as it may occur, if not so much in baton vs baton combat, then at least in self-defence scenarios of baton vs foes either unarmed or armed with shorter weapons *(such as knives)*.

2. To this the outnumbered combatant will react with the same strike on the forehand side *(towards the foe on the backhand side)*, while limiting the approaching step to a lunge with the lead foot

Exercise 14: Free-play integration

1. The combatants making up the group of assailants approach randomly

2. The outnumbered combatant needs, therefore, to read which opponent gets closer first and, consequently, perform the needed engagement strike *(on the backhand or forehand side)*, together with the corresponding follow through strikes

Lesson 8: Combat strategy against 3 – part 1

Goal: To adapt the skill set to a higher number of opponents.

Exercise 15: Review / Introduction

Trainees should start by going over the one against two combat scenario by performing:

1. The engagement strike against the opponent on the forehand side *(by means of a strike on the backhand side)*

2. Three sets of two double strike combinations, where each set is made up by:

    ➤ A first double strike combination in one direction *(towards one of the opponents)*

    ➤ A second double strike combination in which the strikes are split between both opponents *(forward and backwards)*

    Thus, constantly alternating between the two double strike combinations: one combination in one direction and one split in both directions.

> ## Coaching info:
>
> *Earlier it was explained that this combat strategy relies, first and foremost, on the opponents reacting defensively when attacked, out of fear of getting injured (and being injured when they fail to react in such a manner). However, a second note needs to be added regarding trainees' approach to practice.*
>
> *This distance centred combat strategy works out successfully in favour of the outnumbered combatant if all combatants move sensibly at the same speed. In combat this entails everyone performing at maximum speed, which is what naturally occurs. In training, however, getting to that point requires a period of familiarization and correction during which sub-maximal speed is used in order to safely learn this skill set.*
>
> *Nevertheless, special attention needs to be given to the practice at sub-maximal speeds.*
>
> *The trainees making up the group of assailants should look to practice under the intention of shortening distance, in order to attack their opponent whenever possible. However, such martially sound attitude frequently gets trainees to speed up. By increasing speed, trainees end up (1) deceiving themselves by successfully shortening distance against an outnumbered combatant practicing at a slower pace and, additionally, (2) forcing the outnumbered combatant to speed up, which tends to disrupt the lone combatant's learning process. Trainees need to understand that these training drills are for the outnumbered combatant to learn, and their role as "villains" is to create opposition within the speed set by the outnumbered combatant. Once the latter feels comfortable with speeding up, he or she will do so and the others will follow suit, without risking incurring in bad practice.*

Exercise 16: Changing side to the backhand side

1. This time, 3 assailants will approach the lone combatant. They should do so forming a triangle, in order to maximize their chances

of surrounding their opponent

2. For training purposes, the opponent on the forehand side of the outnumbered combatant will approach slightly ahead of the remaining ones

3. To this, the outnumbered combatant will respond with the previously trained strike on the backhand side, while also stepping forward *(diagonally)* with the back leg

4. Having used the engagement strike to also increase distance towards the opponent approaching on the backhand side, the lone combatant performs the double strike combination forward, in the direction of the opponent standing in front of him / her.

    a. Footwork wise, this is performed by moving:

        i. The foot of the backhand side towards the opponent standing in front of the lone combatant, as the first strike is performed

        ii. Followed by a second step with the opposite foot *(passing step)*, when performing the second strike

        iii. Lastly, a spin is performed towards the backside *(moving back the shoulder on the backhand side)*, in order to effectively move to a different side of the triangle while keeping all opponents in the field of view

Exercise 16

1 Starting positions

Foe on the forehand side approaches

2 Pre-emptive strike

3 End of strike

Critical variable:

Strike inside-out, to keep away foe in front

Exercise 16

4 Start of double strike combination

5 End of first strike

6 Transition between strikes

7 End of 2nd strike

Critical variable:

1st step with left leg, followed by right leg

113

5. The outnumbered combatant should, then, perform two additional sets of:

    a. A split double strike combination, in order to keep the opponents at bay

    b. One double strike combination forward in order to change sides. At this stage always towards the foe standing in front of the outnumbered combatant

Upon completion of these 3 sets of two double strike combinations, one returns to the side of the triangle one started from. In doing so, the outnumbered combatant moved through all of the sides of the triangle, taking advantage of the constant openings on the forehand side.

Exercise 16

8 Start of split double strike combination

9 End of strike

10 Start of 2nd strike of the split double strike combination

Critical variable:

Movement flow

Exercise 16

11 End of strike

12 Start of double strike combination forward

13 End of 1st strike

Critical variable:

Strike hands or knee if foes fail to exit

Exercise 16

14
Transition
between
strikes

15 End of
2nd strike

***Critical
variable:***

*Keep all foes
in field of
view*

Lesson 9: Combat strategy against 3 – part 2

Goal:
To conclude the adaptation of the core skill set used in outnumbered combat against three opponents.

Exercise 17: Changing side to the backhand side

1. The outnumbered combatant starts, again, with the engagement strike towards the opponent approaching on the forehand side

2. At the same time that the outnumbered combatant performs the engagement strike to the forehand side:

   ➢ The opponent on the opposite side looks to approach while also drifting to the lone combatant's back

   ➢ The opponent initially standing in front of the outnumbered combatant looks to approach slightly the partner attacked with the engagement strike, in order to close the gap previously used by the outnumbered combatant in moving to a different side of the triangle

3. These manoeuvres, performed as the engagement strike is executed, open up a greater gap on the backhand side of the triangle.

   ➢ Therefore, the outnumbered combatant performs a double strike combination towards the opponent on the backhand side and, at the very end, spins to the backside. In doing so, the outnumbered combatant moves to the side of the triangle initially on the backhand side

➢ The footwork is similar to the one practiced during the previous lesson, in that the foot of the backhand side moves first, followed by a passing step with the other foot. Doing so means that, this time, the double strike combination is performed with a slight lunge during the first strike, followed by a passing step with the back leg *(as the second strike is performed)*.

➢ Note that both steps should be, again, performed straight towards the opponent being attacked *(the one initially on the backhand side)*, and not to the middle of the side of the triangle one is moving towards

Exercise 17

1 End of initial pre-emptive strike

2 Start of double strike combination

3 End of 1st strike

Critical variable:

Lunge with left leg

Exercise 17

4 Transition between strikes

5 End of 2nd strike

6 Rotation of upper body

Critical variable:

After lunge, step with right leg

4. Upon finishing the movement to a different side, the outnumbered combatant should immediately perform a split double strike

combination, in order to keep the opponents at bay

5. Then, the outnumbered combatant should perform two additional sets of:

> A double strike combination in the same direction in order to change sides, at this stage always towards the backhand side

> A split double strike combination to keep the opponents at bay

6. In doing so, three changes of side are completed in the direction of the backhand side of the outnumbered combatant, with the latter returning to the side of the triangle he or she started from

Exercise 17

7 Squaring off with foe at the back

8 End of 1st strike,
of split double strike combination

Exercise 17

9 End of 2nd strike, *of double split strike combination*

10 1st strike of double strike combination forward, *to change sides*

11 Transition between strikes

Critical variable:

Move straight towards foe

Exercise 17

12 Square off with foe on the left

13 Release of 1st strike, *of split double strike combination*

14 End of strike

Critical variable:

Punish hands and knees

Exercise 17

15 Release of 2nd strike, *of split double strike combination*

16 End of strike

17 1st strike of double strike combination forward, *to change sides*

Critical variable:

Lunge with left leg

Exercise 17

18 Start of double strike combination

19 Transition between strikes

20 End of 2nd strike

Critical variable:

Step in with right leg, and keep all foes in field of view

Exercise 18: Engagement on the backhand side

Repeat exercises 16 and 17, while performing the engagement strike towards the opponent on the backhand side *(by means of an inside-out strike from the forehand side)*.

As already trained, this initial strike should be followed with a strike towards the opponent on the forehand side, together with a lunge in the latter's direction *(and, sometimes, also half a step with the non-dominant leg)*.

From the end of this two strike engagement strategy, repeat the three changes of side towards the forehand side *(exercise 16)* and the three changes of side towards the backhand side *(exercise 17)*.

Exercise 18

1 Starting position, *foe on the left approaches first*

2 Start of pre-emptive strike to the backhand side

3 End of strike

Critical variable:

Inside-out strike

Exercise 18

4 Start of strike to the forehand side, *lunging with right leg*

5 End of strike

6 Start of change of side *(ex: forward)*

Critical variable:

Flow & Variability

Exercise 19: Free-play application

1. The group of three assailants moves freely, both in their approach and throughout the exchange

2. The outnumbered combatant needs, therefore, to read the development of combat and react according to the rationale previously trained, depending on:

   a. Which opponent is the first to get within pre-emptive striking reach

   b. Which opening is greater at each point in time, when choosing to move to a different side of the triangle _(which occurs each time one strikes to the forehand side)_

Lesson 10: Dealing with knife wielding opponents and grapplers

Goal: To apply the previously trained skill set to self-defence settings.

Introductory note

When squaring off against each other, knives and batons have both strengths and weaknesses. The traits most relevant to training are:

➢ Batons supply users with a reach advantage

➢ Strikes with sharp knives:

      ☞ Do not need to rely on performing high impact blows that require high range of motion. This adds striking actions of reduced range of motion to the list of strikes one needs to be wary of

      ☞ Their ability to cut through the skin and, hence, reach blood vessels, demands great respect and attention *(whereas batons are most effective in striking at bones and joints)*

Exercise 20: Strategy for using batons vs knives

1. Upon being presented with a knife combatant, the baton combatant should switch to a starting position with the weapon placed pointing backwards over the shoulder *(forehand side)*. This adaptation of the starting position allows for the baton combatant to shorten the range of motion of his or her strikes, and thus have an easier time coping with the speed of a knife combatant

2. The knife combatant feeds a strike to the baton combatant

    a. On the following photos the knife strike is from the shoulder. However, one can also hold the weapon forward and look to close distance by keeping the arm menacingly extended forward

> ### Coaching info:
>
> *Given the reach advantage of the baton, it is possible that some might think of stepping back with a strike to the body of the knife combatant. It is my understanding that, in performing such strikes, the baton combatant may end up getting cut on the forearm, which renders such strategy unadvisable.*

3. The baton combatant should look to distance him or herself in order to preserve distance and, additionally, strike the hand of the knife combatant

Exercise 20

2 Start of distancing step

3 Release of counter strike, *with baton*

4 Counter on foe's hand

Critical variable:

Wide starting distance

Exercise 20

1 Starting position

2 Reaction to a knife strike

3 Counter to the foe's body

Critical variable:

Failure to focus on maximizing reach

Exercise 21: Free-play of baton vs knife

Now, the previous drill should be practiced within a free-play context, in which combatants are allowed to move around in order to attempt to manipulate the starting distance in their favour.

Since this will entail having the knife combatant attempting to shorten distance somewhat, the baton combatant will have access to an additional tool:

➢ When confronted with a knife combatant holding the weapon forward and looking to close distance, the baton combatant can strike to the hand before the knife combatant commits to a strike / approach

 ▪ Nevertheless, the baton combatant should do so while expecting skilled knife combatants to remove the hand from the trajectory of the strike, and immediately approach with a strike / trust.

 Consequently, the baton combatant should avoid overcommitting when approaching with such strike and, additionally, be ready to immediately step back and follow the first striking motion with a second strike *(again aimed at the hand of the knife combatant)*

Exercise 22: Outnumbered self-defence free-play preparation – scenario A

1. Facing two opponents with knives and one unarmed opponent looking to grapple, the outnumbered combatant should start by having the unarmed opponent positioned on the backhand side

2. The unarmed opponent should then take the lead in approaching, to which the outnumbered combatant should react with a pre-emptive strike to the knee

   ➤ The outnumbered combatant should make sure the strike is to the knee, thus avoiding head strikes to such foes. Chances are that the grappler will look to close distance by protecting the head, especially if a winter coat happens to be part of the equation.

Exercise 22

1 Starting positions

2 Pre-emptive strike to foe on the right

3 Targeting head, *less reliable*

4 Targeting knee, *more reliable*

- Should the outnumbered combatant commit to a high strike, and only then notice that the opponent is approaching while covering the head, the strike should be redirected to the hands.

Exercise 23: Outnumbered self-defence free-play preparation – scenario B

1. Building up on the previous scenario, the outnumbered combatant follows the first strike by shifting his or her attention to the other foes

2. As the assailant on the forehand side of the outnumbered combatant looks to approach with a *(knife)* strike, the outnumbered combatant strikes to this opponent's hand

Exercise 23

1 End position of pre-emptive strike

2 Knife attack from the left

3 Strike to the hand of knife attacker

Critical variable:

Preservation of distance

Exercise 24: Outnumbered self-defence free-play preparation – scenario C

1. The first two assailants attacked by the outnumbered combatant[14] distance themselves in order to avoid getting hit

2. For training purposes, the outnumbered combatant moves to the side of the triangle initially on the backhand side, as the grappler presents less danger than the knife wielding opponents

---

Coaching info:

This latest training setting introduced the important concept of adapting one's skill set to the conditions at hand.

Hence, instead of merely moving towards the greater opening (as done in the introductory drills), free play application of this skill set should see the trainees also taking into account information such as the weapon held by each opponent, the location of one's potential escape route, individual traits of each opponent (weaker one, leader, etc).

---

3. As the outnumbered combatant follows up the change of side with a strike to the assailant initially standing in front of him / her, this strike is directed to the hand of the second knife assailant *(who also tries to land a strike with the knife)*

---

[14] The one on the backhand side and the one on the forehand side.

Exercise 24

1 Starting position

2 Reaction to approach of foe on the backhand side

3 Foe steps back to avoid strike

Critical variable:

Timing the pre-emptive strike

Exercise 24

4 Strike to the hand of foe on the forehand side

5 Foe avoids strike, *by stepping back*

6 Transition towards unarmed foe, *starting with a lunge*

Critical variable:

Spot the best opening

Luís Preto, MSc

Exercise 24

7 Follow lunge with passing step

8 Transition between strikes

9 End of second strike

Critical variable:

Move straight towards foe

145

Exercise 24

10 Square off with foe approaching from behind

11 Release of uppercut to foe's hand

12 Hand strike

Critical variable:

Keeping the lead & distance

4. Repeat the exercise with the assailant who was previously getting hit safely avoiding the strike by means of a distancing step *(so that the trainee also learns how to avoid the strike, instead on only learning how to get hit)*

Exercise 25: Outnumbered self-defence free-play

Enjoy the playfulness of free sparring, while looking to detect the occasional possibilities to apply the scenarios previously practiced.

Such practice should develop while respecting the martially sound balance between wishing to attack and being highly zealous of one's own physical integrity _(especially when playing the role of an assailant)_. To promote such balance, it helps establishing that assailants get removed from the game each time they get hit.

On the other hand, strikes worthy of such exclusion from the game should be mainly _(or even exclusively)_ strikes on the hands, knees and head – in order to promote effective targeting by the outnumbered combatant.

Final words

After 10 lessons, made up by 25 drills, this tutorial on multiple opponent combat with one handed weapons has reached its end.

It is my hope that, from a martial standpoint, the contents made sense. Additionally, highlighting the critical components and context of the techniques hopefully proved to be an effective learning approach as well.

In the future, other tutorials will for sure follow, such as an introduction to one on one combat with blunt weapons *(batons / staves)*.

Until then, questions and comments pertaining either this tutorial or training opportunities can be sent to:

traininganswers@outlook.com

I hereby extend you all my most sincere wishes of well-being, and the continuation of a most enjoyable martial experience.

Luís Preto
(September 2016)

STUDY MATERIAL

Coaching sciences

Discount code available on final pages

Appendix:
Left-handed photos

Exercise 4
Solo demo

1 Starting position

2 Transition of weapon to backhand side

3 Start of swing on backhand side

Exercise 4
Solo demo

4 Start of diagonal step forward with back leg

5 Release of strike

6 End of strike & approach

o

o

**Exercise 4
Partner
demo**

1 Starting
positions

2 Foe on
forehand
side
approaches

3 Start of
pre-emptive
strike

***Critical
variable:***

*Timing strike
with
approach of
opponent*

4 Release of pre-emptive strike towards foe on forehand side

5 End of strike & approach

Critical variable:

Performing an inside-out strike

Exercise 5
Solo demo

1 End position of 1st strike

2 Squaring off with opposite foe

3 Release of 1st strike

4 Transition between strikes

Exercise 5
Solo demo

5 Release of
2nd strike

6 End of 2nd
strike

7 Squaring
off with
other foe

8 Release of
1st strike,
*of double
strike
combination*

Exercise 5
Solo demo

9 1st strike

10 Transition between strikes

11 Release of 2nd strike

12 End of double strike combination

Exercise 5
Partner
demo

1 Release of
1st strike, *of*
double
strike
combination

2 End of 1st
strike

3 Transition
between
strikes

4 Release of
2nd strike

**Exercise 5
Partner
demo**

5 End of 2nd
strike

6 Squaring
off with
other foe

7 Release of
strike to
opposite foe

8 Transition
between
strikes

***Critical
variable:***

*Anticipate
strikes from
opponents*

Exercise 6
Solo demo

1 End of initial pre-emptive strike

2 Release of strike towards opposite foe

3 End of strike, and interruption of approaching step

4 Squaring off with opposite foe

Exercise 6
Solo demo

5 Release of strike in the direction opposite to the 1st

6 End of strike

7 Squaring off with opposite foe

8 Release of 1st strike, *of double strike combination*

Exercise 6
Solo demo

9 Transition
between
strikes

10 Release
of 2nd strike

11 End of 2nd
strike,
*of double
strike
combination*

**Exercise 6
Partner
demo**

1 End of
initial pre-
emptive
strike

2 Release of
strike
towards foe
on the left

3 End of
strike

4 Release of
strike in
opposite
direction

**Exercise 6
Partner
demo**

5 End of
strike

6 Release of
1st strike
towards foe
on the left

6 Release of
1st strike
towards foe
on the left

7 End of
strike

8 Transition
between
strikes

Exercise 6
Partner
demo

9 End of 2nd
strike

10 Release
of strike
towards foe
on the right

11 End of
strike

12 Surprise
strike
towards on
the left

Exercise 6
Partner
demo

13 Release
of 1st strike

14 End of
strike

15
Transition
between
strikes

16 End of
2nd strike

Exercise 10
Solo demo

1 Starting position

2 First phase of strike, *with approaching step (using back leg)*

3 End of strike

Critical variable:

Diagonal step, to move away from other foe

**Exercise 10
Partner
demo**

1 Starting
position,
*foe on the
backhand
side
approaches*

2 Pre-
emptive
strike

3 End of
strike

***Critical
variable:***

*Timing
approach by
foes,
strike hand
if reachable*

About the author

The author, Luís Preto, holds an undergraduate degree in physical education and two masters in sport sciences (sports teaching methodologies and coaching).

Additionally, he is a Jogo do Pau instructor, a certified wrestling coach, a black belt in karate and a certified fitness instructor, endurance specialist and youth coach specialist by the International Sport Sciences Association.

In looking to share his thoughts on how to effectively coach both sports in general and martial arts in particular, he has been focused on developing new coaching / teaching concepts. Such concepts, initially gathered under the designation of "Preto martial arts", have recently evolved into the more fitting designation of *"Training Answers"*.

Already an author of several books, Luís Preto has recently also collaborated in the making of two DVDs, and has several other training materials in the works.

STUDY MATERIAL:

Details & Discounts

Tactical skill

COMBAT TACTICS:
Decision making in weapon based martial arts[15]

A context centred combat blueprint which covers:

☞ Delivery of the first strike

☞ Selection of defensive reactions

☞ Awareness of counter striking options

☞ Management of long exchanges

Regarding **defensive guidelines**, you will access a systematization of parries into **two parrying systems**, plus input on how to choose between them according to:

☞ **One's position:**

✓ Starting position

✓ Upon finishing a strike

☞ **The dominant side of one's foe:**

✓ Right-handed foes

✓ Left handed foes

---

[15] 20% discount code – ZBB55D9G, order through www.createspace.com (store section)

TESTIMONIALS

"Super clear demo, great DVD concept, fabulous editing and just great advice on combat training.

It is a must-have for anyone who wishes to take combat training to the next level. I have watched several times and it still keeps teaching me new tricks. Great value for money....it is and hour and a half of pure combat insight!!!"

Peter Archer

"Therefore, the material in the video addresses the options, problems and solution in the sector of offense, defense, counter attacking etc. Still, that is not the best part! For me the absolute treat of this presentation are the chapters on Combat management, Decision pyramid for selecting countering options, and Guiding rationale for the counters with double-handed weapons."

Dragan Milojevic,
Systema and Filipino martial arts instructor

"I've seen a lot of DVD`s and it`s the first time I`ve seen a DVD with everything one needs, from beginner to advance, in the craft of using weapons: strategy, tactics and techniques are everywhere, but the way to put it together takes time and pain. Luis Preto makes those bridges for you – gives you a «decision pyramid» and accelerates your thought. It`s up to you to put it into play."

Pedro Silva,
Head FMA instructor for FMA-Portugal

COACHING COMBAT TACTICS:

Counter attack selection[16]

This book simplifies the training of all fencing (weapon) arts by tackling both:

☞ The subject of contents (What to teach)
☞ Its pedagogy (How to teach).

This is done by sharing concepts, games & drills that easily teach how to choose one's counter according to:

1. Number of opponents
2. Traits of weapons:
    a. Bladed /blunt
    b. With and without hand guard
    c. Single or double handed

3. Having greater, lesser or the same reach
4. Type of parry performed
5. Quality of footwork

An innovative and helpful document in making combat tactical awareness easier to teach / learn.

---

[16] 20% discount code – ZBB55D9G, order through www.createspace.com (store section)

Jogo do Pau

FROM BATTLEFIELD TO DUELING:

The evolution of Jogo do Pau[17]

Lessons from a historical fencing system that resisted the test of time

Jogo do Pau's structured curriculum, product of an unbroken lineage of several centuries of practice, can be a helpful blueprint for HEMA.

This DVD presents the evolution technique and tactics as an adaptation to different combat circumstances, culminating in the improved selection of:

1. Starting position
2. Parrying technique
3. Defensive footwork
4. Counter attack selection
5. Striking technique

BONUS MATERIAL:
A systematization of German longsword combat tactics, for improved sparring performance.

---

[17] 20% discount code – ZBB55D9G, order through www.createspace.com (store section)

TESTIMONIALS

"A good understanding of the interrelationships between guards, attacks and parries helps in creating a good perception of timing and distance. In such the DVD proves useful to practitioners and instructors of weapon arts, both modern and historical: the mentioned correlations are well explained and lead to simple pointers in the making of tactical decisions. The pros and cons of stances and attacks are clearly demonstrated and in addendum illustrated in relation to the German school of the longsword."

**Alwin Goethals,
Lead instructor of SWARTA (HEMA)**

"Overall, Luis is a very clear speaker and a precise, professional instructor and a skilled stick fighter. On top of this, his pedagogic background and skills are strongly coming out in this DVD, that I certainly recommend to any western martial artists (well, any martial artists). Plus, the location of the video is certainly evocative and just about right."

**Marco Quarta,
HEMA instructor**

"As always, Luis anticipates training concerns and both mechanical and technical questions, providing answers and solutions to most of the issues that arise in training."

**Roland Cooper,
HEMA instructor at Academie Duello**

Teaching / Coaching

TECHNIQUE & TACTICAL SKILL:

A practical guide for coaches, parents and athletes[18]

This book bridges the gap between research on sports-teaching & the practical day-to-day work of teaching sport skills … all in all, teaching is made simple and effective by sharing great insight into:

☞ What makes up movement software
☞ How motor skills develop as an adaptation to opponent's traits, game rules & one's body image
☞ The training of psychological variables
☞ A teaching system that optimizes:
  ▪ Motivation & concentration
  ▪ Coordination & Memorization
  ▪ Transfer from drills to game performance

The way these topics are covered using concepts and teaching examples, reading this book easily fits everyone's previous knowledge and has an immediate positive impact on future teaching endeavours.

---

[18] 20% discount code – ZBB55D9G, order through www.createspace.com (store section)

TESTIMONIALS

"After explaining how our movement software works, Luis Preto gave us way to teach new technics in a tactical environment, and every time it is based on pretty good example. For me this is a must-have for all martial-art teacher"

Aurel,
HEMA instructor

"By reading this book you will learn how to use most appropriate methods for the skill level of your students and then maximise the retention of their improved motor skills."

...

"In short this is a book that I cannot recommend enough to anyone wanting to improve their coaching ability."

...

"Obviously I am interested in the coaching of martial arts, however the information contained within this book will benefit anyone involved in coaching any physical skill or sport."

Paul Genge,
Systema instructor

Made in United States
North Haven, CT
17 February 2024

48853845R00104